THE KINGDOM OF GOD AND THE HUMAN RACE

An expanded understanding of God's heart for the human race.

BISHOP FRANK F ROSEWELT

2020

The Kingdom God and The Human Race: An expanded understanding of God's heart for the human race.

ISBN : 978-976-96536-0-3

Book Cover Design : Anna Snider (http://annerlaine.com/mywork/)

Publisher : The Publisher's Notebook Limkited

Email : **thepublishersnotebook@gmail.com**

Telephone : 876 331 0727

Contents

Foreword

Bishop Dr. Frank Rosewelt, is a true Apostle. He is a global and regional gift to the Body of Christ.

In this book, **The Kingdom of God and the Human Race,** Bishop Rosewelt speaks with a clear understanding, and gives an accurate theology of the Kingdom of God.

It is evident that he has received a divine encounter to preach, teach and evangelize using Kingdom principles, in this nation and beyond. He understands both the principle and concept of the Church as the agent of the Kingdom of God to bring lasting reformation to mankind.

As a proponent of the Kingdom for the last forty years, he has maintained a vibrant local church, weekly televised broadcasts, and radio ministry.

This truly is his literary season and as a prophetic voice to the nations, this work is relevant for kingdom advancement and lifestyle. I therefore recommend this work as a must read to every believer in pursuit of Kingdom upgrade.

Bishop Dr. Neville Owens (JP)
Marriage Officer
President of the Independent Churches of Jamaica
Apostle and Kingdom Proclaimer

Preface

Knowledge continues to grow at an exponential rate. Knowledge was estimated to be doubling between one and two years at the beginning of the 21st century. By 2017 knowledge is estimated to be doubling every twelve hours. Just to bring us a little closer home, communication devices have changed significantly in the past two years from analog cell phones to digital mobile phone to smartphones. Life has never been the same since the introduction of, and global availability of the cell phones to society.

All things are parallel, whatever is manifest in the seen material world has long before been operating in the invisible spiritual realm. The angel said to Daniel, close the book until the time of the end when men will be going and coming, and knowledge shall increase (Daniel 12: 4).

In an age of migration and immigration, tourism and social upheaval, when knowledge shall increase according to the angel, its an indication of the end.

We are definitely at the end of the age as seen by multiple indicators. One primary indicator as spoken by our Lord is that, this gospel of the Kingdom shall be preached into all the world as a witness to all nation then the end shall come (Matthew 24:14).

I was pressed in my spirit to write this book as I saw multiple indications of the end of the world system as we know it, and the Christian church oblivious of the gospel of the Kingdom of God. I grew up in a church culture of which escaping from earth to heaven was the hope of the human race.

This widely propagated teaching and preaching has left the Church ignorant of the great plans and purposes of God's heart for the human race and by extension the universe.

If you are just a casual reader of the New Testament portion of the Bible it cannot escape your attention that the theme, the frequent mention of the Kingdom of God by the Lord Jesus is what dominates His teaching. It was His passion, His assignment and His reason for coming. (Luke 4:42 – 43).

One mostly overlooked scripture is recorded in Acts 1:3. After His resurrection He was seen by His disciples over a period of forty days and He continued His teaching, the Bible said, about the Kingdom of God. He did not teach about speaking in tongues, it was not a discourse on methods of baptism, day of worship or holiness. He continued to teach them about the Kingdom of God.

How could we have missed why He came? How did we detour to go to heaven to live when that is not supported by scripture? When did God say, "come let us make man in our image and our likeness and let them come to heaven to live with us?" If we should go back to the beginning of man's introduction into the earth you will notice he came into the earth realm with a kingdom. His ability to dominate and to rule was an intrinsic part of his nature (Genesis 1:26-28).

It is an indictment against the church if we say we love Him, we worship Him, we preach Him as Lord and Savior, we sing about Him, but we cannot say why He came and what was His message. The wise man Solomon wrote:

> *Proverbs 25:2 It is the glory of God to conceal a thing: but the honour of kings is to search out a matter.*

I would beseech you to rise to the dignity of your calling and investigate the matter of Christ Jesus and His kingdom. I guarantee you that it will revolutionize your life and ministry.

Dr Frank F. Rosewelt

Acknowledgments

Bishop Neville Owens, my mentor and friend whose passion for the gospel of the Kingdom of God is inspiring. To members of International Worship Center who place constant demands on the anointing to produce fresh revelation about the mysteries of the kingdom.

To my friend Robert Whyte who unflaggingly urged me to write this book to the intent the Christian community would not be ignorant of the gospel that Jesus Christ preached.

The trailblazers in the twentieth century who have written about the Kingdom of God that have inspired me.

Introduction

It has been far too long that man has been merely existing and not truly living. It is crucial to note that the apex of God's creative ingenuity is man, not oil neither minerals. Therefore, the entity of man is more than just a personality, he is an embodiment of enormous possibilities. He is the only being created in God's image and after His likeness that has a clear assignment from the infallible word of God in the earth. Clearly from this precedence it can be concluded that the first man, Adam, had the nature of God as he was created in God's image and according to His likeness.

It is very important that we understand that Adam was given a Kingdom to rule and enforce the rights and privileges within the boundaries of Gods directives in the earth. The fact that Adam was given dominion is speaking to authority to reign, to subdue or subjugate. On this basis, it's imperative to establish that God did not give him a religion, as Adam was the son of God which speaks to relationship not a religious person. Adam's disobedience to the directive had actually ceded the throne to Satan, so there was an erosion in the originality of God's plan for man. This resulted in a loss of relationship with the Father as he was automatically disconnected from this awesome Kingdom; but God had an unstoppable program which was fulfilled in the fullness of time. Hallelujah!

This glorious redemption to the devious scheme of the devil's tactic was actualized through Jesus Christ, the last Adam who came and redeemed man by reinstating him to his original position. It is extremely important that thorough comprehension of the methodologies of God is understood, thus we do not risk misrepresenting His pristine divinity and sovereignty. Ignorance is responsible for man's vulnerability to the deceptive devices of the enemy. In fact, in Hebrew the word for darkness is the same as the word for ignorance. Truth is the antidote for deception and accurate knowledge destroys ignorance. The believer must be aware that there are two worlds which are contending with each other which are the Kingdom of Darkness and the Kingdom of Light. Anyone who is born again and professes Jesus Christ as Lord is qualified as a citizen of the Kingdom of God with inherent rights and privileges to impact the earth with the Government of God.

If you can comprehend the profundity of this scenario you will discover that this is absolutely majestic in its conception and all-encompassing in its scope. Jesus Christ came with a Kingdom mandate to empower man to function and represent God in the earth. Man is entrusted with dominion and carries a superior system that has keys for specific circumstance geared towards specific results in the Kingdom. The Kingdom of God here is a compendium of infinite possibilities.

In this book, **The Kingdom of God and The Human Race**, Dr. Rosewelt seeks to unravel several corner stones and establish fundamental tenets, that are vital to serve as a radical alternative to the ills of today's religious marketplace. I believe the content presented is rather potent and will develop the faculty of perception where understanding the systems and structures of the Kingdom will be realized. I urge you to invite the Holy Spirit as your senior partner in this appointment with destiny, where Dr. Rosewelt will be examining some pivotal concepts through the keen lenses of wisdom with microscopic clarity to foster spiritual empowerment. I am excited about this...are you ready?

The resounding "yes" I hear is staggering at best. As you invite the Holy Spirit to open the eyes of your understanding to the information provided in this book, I pray that you will grasp the very essence of the dimensions of Kingdom reality. If you are born again, you are a citizen of the Kingdom of God with rights and privileges. This multifaceted dimension of the Kingdom of God is indeed within you. We may not be in earthly political government, but we are in power.

It is time to unleash the Kingdom within you, don't be afraid of it, experience it. Don't be intimated by it, explore it. Seize this upgrade you have been waiting for, receive divine enablement and spiritual empowerment now for the higher calling in Jesus Christ.

Pastor Robert Whyte, J.P.
Senior Pastor, Bethel Embassy International Ministries.

THE KINGDOM OF GOD AND THE HUMAN RACE

The Kingdom of God and The Human Race

1. The Meaning of Kingdom

He was dressed in a most rugged fashion. To the average onlooker, he seemed far removed from the society and unconcerned about the social graces of his countrymen. It would appear as if he was offering a counterculture. But John the Baptist would not be considered trendy by the Romans who occupy the land of the Jews, neither would he, in the way he was dressed, impress any of the other nationalities that dwell in Palestine. But to the Jews John's attire was sending a strong prophetic message. A promise of God from the past of an iconic personage who had brought about a mighty awakening of the worship of Jehovah in Israel - the prophet Elijah. God has spoken by the prophet Malachi that he would send the messenger:

> ***Malachi 3:1*** *- "...I will send my messenger, and he shall prepare the way before me:"*

The messenger is the same whom Isaiah had foretold, whose words John uses:

> ***Isaiah 40:3*** *- "The voice of one crying in the wilderness, prepare ye the way of the Lord, make straight in the desert a highway for our God".*

This messenger was identified as John the Baptist who came in the spirit and power of Elijah. The Angel of the Lord spoke to Zechariah concerning John's assignment

> ***Luke 1:17*** - *And he shall go before him in the spirit and power of Elias, to turn the hearts of the fathers to the children, and the disobedient to the wisdom of the just; to make ready a people prepared for the Lord.*

John did get the attention of his countrymen. They flocked to hear him and be baptized by him. He had a message that had long being anticipated. The message of the Kingdom of God. He challenged them to repent for the Kingdom of God is at hand. One would believe that John would be questioned about his message. The questions came with rigid interrogation, but it was not about the message since the nation was in high expectation for the kingdom, the questions were about the messenger.

> ***John 1:19-23 (ASV)*** - *And this is the witness of John, when the Jews sent unto him from Jerusalem priests and Levites to ask him, Who art thou? And he confessed, and denied not; and he confessed, I am not the Christ (Messiah). And they asked him, What then? Art thou Elijah? And he saith, I am not. Art thou the prophet? And he answered, No. They said therefore unto him, Who art thou? that we may give an answer to them that sent us. What sayest thou of thyself? He said, I am the voice of one crying in the wilderness, Make straight the way of the Lord, as said Isaiah the prophet.*

According to Jesus, John the Baptist was the greatest man to be ever born of a woman.

> ***Matthew 11:11*** - *Verily I say unto you, Among them that are born of women there hath not risen a greater than John the*

Baptist: notwithstanding he that is least in the kingdom of heaven is greater than he.

Let's give some consideration to Jesus' statement. To the nation of Israel, and I mean the entire nation, Moses was the great man of the time. The great Hebrew national hero, leader, author, law-giver and prophet. Then what about Elijah, the prophet of fire and great reformer? Elijah brought about a reformation at a time when the worship of Jehovah was threatened by Baal worship under the rulership of Ahab and Jezebel. There are so many others who have made significant contributions to the nation that could be referred to as great; King David and Solomon his son are two examples. Outside of the Jewish nation others who were considered great were also born of women.

This statement of Jesus was highly controversial to the Jews. But, then, Jesus was at the time and still is one of the most controversial persons the world has ever seen or heard of.

Matthew 11:11a - "Among them born of women there has not risen a greater than John the Baptist,..."

To the Jews and to the rest of the world today this is a polemic statement of such magnitude that cannot be understood outside of a perspective of the Kingdom of God. Then He added,

Matthew 11:11b. -"notwithstanding he that is least in the kingdom of heaven is greater than he".

Least in the kingdom is greater than John? Among them born of women none greater than John? But the man in God's kingdom is greater than John. Why? Because John was of the old system. A system that has failed because of the weakness of the flesh. John introduced a new dispensation; and that the old one, under which the prophets and the law of Moses were the guide, was closed when he preached that the Kingdom of Heaven was at hand. Jesus further added,

> ***Matthew 11:13*** *- "For all the prophets and the law prophesied until John"..*

After John the Baptist, the dispensation of the Kingdom of God was introduced in the earth realm by God for the benefit of the human race.

Now watch this very carefully because it's among the most important statements you have ever heard. People who are in the kingdom are not referred to as "born of women" but born of water and the Spirit, they are 'born again". That means they are regenerated and carry the nature of God or a spiritual DNA was introduced in them that produced new patterns of behavior.

The greatest human being to walk this earth is Jesus Christ, the great God, the creator who came to restore his creation to original purpose, design and intention. Thus, the Kingdom of God/Heaven was introduced by John and confirmed by Jesus as an authentic move of God in the earth for the benefit of the entire human race.

2. THE NATURE OF THE KINGDOM OF GOD

The Kingdom of God is universal yet it is individual. It is present, yet it is the future. It is unseen, yet is seen.

1) The Kingdom of God is spiritual. It is an unseen invisible spiritual reality that has power to invade the visible material creation. It brings salvation and deliverance to people, healing sicknesses and creating order out of disorder.

2) The Kingdom is actual, it is presently existing and operating, as a reality on the earth. You can be impacted by its power, see its activities, and experience its influences.

3) The Kingdom is ideal, it is to come, as a visible glorious government in the universe. It is a historic event to occur some time in the near future. The material universe will be consummated by this glorious spiritual reality. Romans 8: 18-22. 2 Peter 3:12-13.

4) People are related to the Kingdom in three (3) ways;

    a.   they can see it (that is its effect and experience its influence),

b. they can enter it through the new birth, and

c. they will inherit it at the end of the age.

(John 3: 3 -8) Jesus answered and said unto him, Verily, verily, I say unto thee, Except a man be born again, he cannot see the Kingdom of God. ⁴ Nicodemus saith unto him, How can a man be born when he is old? can he enter the second time into his mother's womb, and be born? ⁵ Jesus answered, Verily, verily, I say unto thee, Except a man be born of water and of the Spirit, he cannot enter into the Kingdom of God. ⁶ That which is born of the flesh is flesh; and that which is born of the Spirit is spirit. ⁷ Marvel not that I said unto thee, Ye must be born again. ⁸ The wind bloweth where it listeth, and thou hearest the sound thereof, but canst not tell whence it cometh, and whither it goeth: so is every one that is born of the Spirit.

Many like Nicodemus in the church are so programmed to live by sight that they are oblivious that man is a triune being. Man is first spirit he possessed a soul and live in a body. The process of regeneration (born again) focuses on man's spirit so that the life of God is restored to him.

INHERITING THE KINGDOM

The Kingdom of God is the inheritance of the saints.

(1 Corinthians 6: 9-10) Know ye not that the unrighteous shall not inherit the Kingdom of God? Be not deceived: neither fornicators, nor idolaters, nor adulterers, nor effeminate, nor abusers of themselves with mankind, ¹⁰ Nor thieves, nor covetous, nor drunkards, nor revilers, nor extortioners, shall inherit the Kingdom of God.

(1 Corinthians 15:50-51) ⁵⁰ Now this I say, brethren, that flesh and blood cannot inherit the Kingdom of God; neither doth corruption inherit incorruption. ⁵¹ Behold, I shew you a mystery; We shall not all sleep, but we shall all be changed,

(Matthew 25:34). *³⁴ Then shall the King say unto them on his right hand, Come, ye blessed of my Father, **inherit** the kingdom prepared for you from the foundation of the world:*

Our objective is not what the Kingdom of God means as it is popularly used today in religious circles; or what we think it means, but what Jesus meant by it.

Firstly, we must understand while the teaching was originally proclaimed by Jesus, the name Kingdom of God did not originate with him. The Kingdom of God begins as a concept in the writings of Moses and the prophets as found in Genesis 1:26-28 and Exodus 19:6. The Psalms are replete with the concept of the Kingdom of God. God is seen as King and supreme ruler. Some examples are:

Psalm 22:28 - For the kingdom is the LORD's: and he is the governor among the nations.

Other references can be found in Psalms 45:6; 103:19; and 145:11-12. There are also examples that can be seen in the books of the prophets —

Isaiah. 9:7 - Of the increase of his government and peace there shall be no end, upon the throne of David, and upon his kingdom, to order it, and to establish it with judgment and with justice from henceforth even for ever. The zeal of the LORD of hosts will perform this.

Daniel 2:44-47 - And in the days of these kings shall the God of heaven set up a kingdom, which shall never be destroyed: and the kingdom shall not be left to other people, [but] it shall break in pieces and consume all these kingdoms, and it shall stand for ever. ⁴⁵ Forasmuch as thou sawest that the stone was cut out of the mountain without hands, and that it brake in pieces the iron, the brass, the clay, the silver, and the gold; the great God hath made known to the king what shall come to pass

> *hereafter: and the dream [is] certain, and the interpretation thereof sure. 46 Then the king Nebuchadnezzar fell upon his face, and worshipped Daniel, and commanded that they should offer an oblation and sweet odours unto him. 47 The king answered unto Daniel, and said, Of a truth [it is], that your God [is] a God of gods, and a Lord of kings, and a revealer of secrets, seeing thou couldest reveal this secret.*

Other related scriptures include Daniel 4:34; 6:26; and 7:13-14, 18, 22, and 27.

The Kingdom of God was not Jesus' idea. He came at the appointed time, when the expectation of the Jews for the Kingdom of God was in a heightened state. Two things happened in the generation before Jesus came. Firstly, due to Roman dominance and oppression the hope of the manifestation of the Kingdom of God was intensified. The Jews sought their deliverance from the kingdom of Rome with the hope that God's kingdom as promised by the prophets would come.

The second is that they believed the Messiah of the kingdom would come with military might and a political agenda, as a result the concept of the kingdom became totally secular and materialistic. For the Jews it was no longer the Kingdom of God but the kingdom of Israel. It would be a Jewish kingdom. Men were now seeking positions and fame, such as James and John who wanted to be on Jesus' right and left hand in the kingdom.

Jesus totally revolutionized the current concept of the kingdom to bring back the original idea of the divine intention, which was God's original plan for the human race to have dominion. That is why

Jesus is always asking the religious leaders one question, *"have you not read…?"* or stating, *"in the beginning it was not so…"*. He came to take us back to the divine purpose of God for the human race.

The most important question to ask is, "what is God's purpose for creating man?"

We have lost sight of our beginning. We are so excited with the present age of information and technology. We pride ourselves with the works of own hands, big cities, smart phones, smart cars, smart cities, space travel that we view the past with skepticism and regard it as primitive. But to lose track of our beginning is to lose all that is fundamental and essential for our existence.

There is a real threat of the knowledge of the purpose of the human race being lost beneath the maze of speculations, unproven theories and conjectures of our collective human wisdom.

The truth of our existence is documented as historic record in a book that most people have a copy of that they never read, understood or believe.

But to lose track of our beginning is to lose all that is fundamental and essential for our existence

This book, the Bible, records the introduction of mankind in the material universe in one profound important statement that revealed his nature and his purpose.

Genesis 1:26 And God said, Let us make man in our image, after our likeness: and let them have dominion over the fish of the sea, and over the fowl of the air, and over the cattle, and over all the earth, and over every creeping thing that creeps upon the earth.

The most astounding aspect of this statement is, nowhere else in the creative narrative was there a mention of the Godhead taking a collective decision on any actions. "Let us" divine consultation is required and wise consideration to execute the crowning act of creation – *"Let us make man."*

There is a real threat of the knowledge of the purpose of the human race being lost beneath the maze of speculations, unproven theories and conjectures of our collective human wisdom.

When man was created, his nature and sphere of influence was determined. Man was given dominion over earth. Man was introduced in the earth with a kingdom.

Jesus took the idea of the kingdom and totally revolutionized it to bring back the original idea of the divine intention, which was God's original plan for the human race to have dominion.

Four important distinctions were made in Jesus' teaching on the kingdom:

1. The kingdom is spiritual not material (John 3:3-8)

2. The kingdom is actual. It is at hand and is presently actively invading the dominion of darkness releasing men and women from enslavement to satanic and demonic power (Matthew 12: 28-29).

3. The kingdom is moral not religious, giving men power to do what is right. It is within you (Luke 17:20)

    Romans 14: 17 - *Greater is he that is in you than he that is in the world.*

4. The kingdom is ideal. It is to come in its fullness at the end of the age as a glorious government in the universe "in power and great glory" (Matthew 24:30; 25: 31-34)

We must try and understand the two stages of the Kingdom of God. It was inaugurated when Jesus came to planet earth and initiated His ministry. The enemy was pulverized at Calvary, as the Bible says in the letter to the Hebrews:

Hebrews 2:14. "through his death He (Christ) destroyed him that has the power of death, that is the devil".

You may wonder why Satan is destroyed yet we still see suffering, sickness, disease, death. Let me draw you an illustration. During World War 2, the enemy was defeated on June 6, 1944 on what is called **D-Day**. The Allied forces invaded Normandy, breaking the back of the enemy and ensuring their total victory. Yet, the war lingered on even though the enemy was defeated. It wasn't until May 7, 1945 (**V-Day**) that the peace treaty was actually signed. Sadly, more people were killed between D-Day and V-Day than any other period of the war. Like that period between D- & V-day, we are living in a period between the inauguration of the Kingdom and the Consummation of the Kingdom. According to the revealed word of God, the consummation of the kingdom is conditioned on the return of the King.

THE RIGHTEOUSNESS OF GOD

Righteousness is a word from the judicial systems, which means to be in right relationship with the governing authority. Jesus said,

> *"seek ye first the Kingdom of God and his righteousness and all other thing will be added unto you."*

Righteousness is not to do something, it is to be something.

The righteousness of God must be understood as God being sovereign declaring you righteous, that is in right relationship with Himself. The only way for man to be righteous before God is by connecting to Jesus Christ as personal Lord and Savior. Righteousness is not to do something it, is to be something.

Righteousness was imputed to Abraham because he believed God. Noah was seen as righteous because of the grace of God. Genesis 7v1. Adam was born righteous. That was his nature. We who are in Christ Jesus were made righteous through the new birth. We were born righteous in the Kingdom of God.

> *Ephesians 4:24. And that ye put on the new man, which after God is created in righteousness and true holiness.*

Regeneration is not about joining a church, and good behavior like no longer cussing and carousing around. By regeneration you have become a new creation. Re-gene-ration means that the "genes" of God is restored to the dead bankrupt spirit of man. We can conclude that the image of God is restored to man, and man by regeneration is restored to the image of God, as in the beginning when God created man (Genesis 1:27).

> ***2 Corinthians 5:17.*** - *If anyone be in Christ he is a new creation,...*

Man was first created as a spirit being before God made a body for man so he could interact in a material universe (Genesis 2:7).

3. A KINGDOM OF RIGHTEOUSNESS

Righteousness is not a word that came from heaven with Jesus. It is a word from the judicial system which means to be upright, sincere, your actions are judged innocent. One meaning is to be in right relationship with the governing authority. If the government deemed you innocent, then you are righteous.

> *Matthew 6:33 Seek ye first the Kingdom of God and His righteousness and all these things will be added unto you.*

Righteousness is a requirement to inherit the Kingdom of God. Notice what the apostle Paul wrote,

> *1 Corinthians 6:9, 10, 'Don't you know that the unrighteous won't inherit the Kingdom of God? Don't make any mistakes about this: Sexually immoral people, idol worshipers, adulterers, gays, men who have sex with men, thieves, greedy people, drunkards, insulters, and extortionists, won't inherit God's Kingdom.' (American English Bible).*

The Kingdom of God is God's work among us. Jesus Christ is the reigning king of God's government. The Kingdom is a present spiritual reality operating in the universe and particularly in His church on earth. All power is given to our Lord in heaven and on earth. There is one outstanding example. Saul of Tarsus, original exterminator was bent on making the church extinct when the great

God made his appearance. It was an all-powerful supernatural appearance. He appeared in the brilliance of light that was above the brightness of the sun. The horses must have been startled by the light and thrown its rider to the ground and that's when he heard the voice,

"Saul, Saul why are you persecuting me". He responded by asking, who are you, Lord? Saul was astounded by the reply. "I am Jesus whom you are persecuting". Acts 9:1-5.

Let us get into the mind of Saul for a moment. "Jesus! The man we had crucified? Jesus! the man we denounced as a mere criminal?" That was his astonishment, THE MAN. If Jesus had said, "I am God whom you are persecuting" the impression would not be as great. We expected God to have made such an appearance as he had done in the past with Moses. But this is the same Jesus that Pilate had ordered scourged and publicly disgraced. He then brought him forth and said, "behold the man." Jesus the man!

No wonder the understanding of God's plans and purpose for the human race by this apostle was so profound. He of all the apostles understood that God was not after a religion. He recalled how he prospered in the Jews religion (Galatians 1:13-14). He prayed that Israel would repent of their religious mindset to become apart of God's global kingdom initiative (Romans 10:1-2).

This brings us to the Holy Spirit.

4. THE HOLY SPIRIT AND THE KINGDOM

Matthew 12:28 - *But if I cast out devils by the Spirit of God, then the kingdom of God is come unto you.*

John 16:13 - *Howbeit when he, the Spirit of truth, is come, he will guide you into all truth: for he shall not speak of himself; but whatsoever he shall hear, that shall he speak: and he will shew you things to come.*

The Holy Spirit is intrinsically connected to the Kingdom of God. The person of the Holy Spirit is one of the basic and essential features that make the kingdom, the Kingdom. This means outside of the Holy Spirit, there can be no Kingdom.

Everything that God undertakes to do in the earth realm and through His Kingdom involves the Holy Spirit. Outside of the Holy Spirit the Kingdom remains inoperative. To restrict and limit the activities of the Holy Spirit in any ministry is to put constraints on the government of God to operate.

We have become more cognizant not only of the role of the Holy Spirit but who He is. The Holy Spirit is God. Divine attributes are ascribed to Him as seen in these scriptures:

Hebrews 9:14 - How much more, then, will the blood of Christ, who through the eternal Spirit offered himself unblemished to God, cleanse our consciences from acts that lead to death,[a] so that we may serve the living God!

Psalm 139: 7-10 - Whither shall I go from thy spirit? or whither shall I flee from thy presence? 8 If I ascend up into heaven, thou art there: if I make my bed in hell, behold, thou art there. 9 If I take the wings of the morning, and dwell in the uttermost parts of the sea; 10 Even there shall thy hand lead me, and thy right hand shall hold me.

2 Corinthians 13:14 - The grace of the Lord Jesus Christ, and the love of God, and the communion of the Holy Ghost, be with you all. Amen.

Remember, every work of God in the earth is connected with the Holy Spirit.

1. We are born again through the agency of the Holy Spirit (John 3:5)

2. Jesus cast out devils by the Holy Spirit: he said, if I by the spirit of God cast out devils then the Kingdom of God is come upon you (Matthew 12:28)

3. Effective prayer is through the Holy Spirit (Romans 8:26)

4. The manifestation of miracles, works of power, and any manifestation of the supernatural has to do with the Holy Spirit, and the Holy Spirit is God.

5. The Holy Spirit has functions of His own in distinct from that of the Father. The Spirit was God in action,

particularly when the action was specific, with a view to accomplishing a particular purpose of God.

6. The Holy Spirit is the manifest presence of God in the earth, He is the Comforter who came when the Son went back to heaven.

John 14:16 - And I will pray the Father, and he shall give you another Comforter, that he may abide with you for ever;

7. While the Son in His humanity was limited to a single geographic locality, the Holy Spirit in His divinity is omni-present.

8. The church has been debating for years whether the Holy Spirit is a person or just a force and an impersonal influence. Some see him as God's power in action and if they could get some of this power, they too could do mighty things. However, if we could see the Holy Spirit as a person, a divine being, a majestic glorious infinitely wise being whom we could give ourselves to that He might use us as He wills, only then we would experience more than power. We would find love unparalleled, joy unspeakable, glory incomprehensible, a comforter, a guide, someone with wise counsel, a friend that sticks closer than a brother, a yoke destroyer and a burden lifter. The Holy Spirit is a person. He feels, can be grieved, gives gifts and other good things.

9. The Holy Spirit is offered to you. To experience the power and influence of the Kingdom of God, the Holy Spirit must be in you. This is one of the most profound statements made by the lord while he was on earth, he said in response to the urging of the religious people of when the Kingdom of God would come. He said the kingdom comes not with observation (that is with outward visible signs) neither will they say look here it is or there it is for behold the Kingdom is within you (Luke 17: 20)

John 14:17 Even the Spirit of truth; whom the world cannot receive, because it sees him not, neither knows him: but ye know him; for he dwells with you, and shall be in you.

Here we find the indwelling Spirit of God revolutionizing the life of those who receive Jesus Christ as savior from a life of sin and bondage, death and condemnation. The apostle Paul wrote in

Romans 8:1 & 2 - "there is therefore now no condemnation to them who are in Christ Jesus who walked not after the flesh but after the Spirit for the law of the Spirit of life in Christ Jesus has made me free from the law of sin and death".

5. THE HOLY SPIRIT

Isaiah 59:19b - When the enemy shall come in like a flood the Spirit of The Lord shall lift up a standard against him.

In other words when the enemy mobilizes his forces the Kingdom of God will suddenly become active to defend you. Why? Because the Holy Spirit carries all the operations of the Kingdom of God.

We can safely infer from this verse that the power and influence to restore order and wholeness to the human race and by extension the universe, is now operating on planet Earth - the Kingdom of God. We can safely say also that without the Holy Spirit God's power will not operate and his glory will not manifest.

> Outside of the Holy Spirit, there can be no dominion or rulership, authority or power. The governing influence of the Kingdom of Heaven on earth is the Holy Spirit.

If Jesus had said "repent for the kingdom will be here someday," I could understand the present position the church holds in respect to the Kingdom of God, that is to get saved and then wait for the Kingdom to come. However, Jesus' life and teaching shows that the Kingdom had arrived, or it is here now in the power of the Holy Spirit.

❖ The Holy Spirit is essentially connected to the operations of the Kingdom of God. The Holy Spirit is one of the basic and essential features that make the Kingdom of God, the Kingdom: This means outside of the Holy Spirit, there can be no dominion or rulership, authority or power. The governing influence of the kingdom of heaven on earth is the Holy Spirit.

❖ By the Holy Spirit the environment of the Kingdom of God is created: in this environment power is released, captives are set free, chains are shattered and fetters are loosed: demonic and satanic influences are suspended giving opportunity for people to be saved, delivered and sanctified. It is in this realm of influence and environment that angels are released to bring deliverance, and sign and wonders take place.

❖ Who is the Holy Spirit? The Holy Spirit is God. Everything that God (the Father) who is the original source of all that there is, undertakes to do in the earth realm involves the Holy Spirit.

❖ Who is the Holy Spirit? The Holy Spirit is God. We first heard of him in Genesis 1:2. *Ruach Elohim* - the word for Wind, Breath, Spirit, in the Hebrew is Ruach, in the Greek it is *Pneuma*.

❖ God breathed into Adam the breath of life. God's Spirit was now in man to give life to what was made from dust.

What had affected and brought stupendous and astounding changes, bringing order and intelligence in the universe was now in man to animate, invigorate and energize. God didn't breathe breath into Adam, He breathed "the breath of life". What was put in Adam was significantly different from lower class of animal life. He had the Breath of life or the Spirit of Life means that Christ was put into Adam.

Romans 8:1 - *there is therefore now no condemnation to them who are in Christ Jesus, who walk not after the flesh but after the spirit, for the law of the Spirit of life in Christ Jesus..."*

Eternal life is not so much about long life, it is about a quality of life that cannot be eroded by time, because eternal life is a person. Our great God and savior made this profound statement while on earth,

John 11:25-26 - *I am the resurrection and the life ...,*

❖ The Spirit gave birth to Christ in Adam. Adam must now feed on the Word of God for his life (which is Christ) to come to fullness. This method of sustenance and nourishment for Adam's development God himself undertakes to do. Therefore, God met with Adam to speak into his spirit. "For man was not created to live by bread alone but by every word that proceeds out of the mouth of God". And if you recall, God's words are spirit and they are life.

Job 6:63 - *It is the spirit that quicken; the flesh profits nothing: the words that I speak unto you, they are spirit, and they are life.*

Everything was going good for Adam, he was developing and maturing into the image of God. He was placed in a culture for his development and maturity, and to transmit that culture to other places in the earth realm bringing order, structure, intelligence and governmental authority.

He was meeting with God and feeding on every word that proceeded out of the mouth of God. He was not yet fully developed and " filled with all the fullness of God" which is the glory of God (Ephesians 3:19, Romans 3:23). The process was compromised when he sinned.

When Adam sinned two things happen simultaneously, the Holy Spirit left, and he instantly died spiritually. Secondly, his body was contaminated by the fruit he ate, and it was only a matter of time before he died physically. He ingested a virus into his body systems that reverse the process of growth and development. A body that was created to live forever with the life of God animating it. Our bodies are now referred to as vile corrupt body of death.

The Holy Spirit on the day of Pentecost was given or restored to the human race, through the life, death and resurrection of our l.ord Jesus. The sound came from heaven. God breathe one more time as He did in Genesis. Winds are known to blow horizontally not vertically. This particular wind came down from heaven, came from God.

In the previous dispensation (the Old Testament) the Spirit came upon people to increase their ability, to carry out supernatural works, the prophets were carried beyond themselves to see events and important significant changes that would take place in the nations. The Holy Spirit in the new dispensation however operates significantly different from the old.

His operations and functions revealed occurrences, manifest powers that are beyond the ability of the human agency in whom he dwells, of which, if closely correlated could only be attributed to the divine invasion of a supernatural power. This power corrects the dysfunctional state of man and restores him to an awareness of the glorious presence of God, with its attended spiritual environment.

6.   The Great Shift

Hebrews 1:1 reminds us that an unprecedented shift has taken place in the way God is dealing with people on the planet. In the past there was a degree of anointing for prophetic utterances, insight and acts of God to the nation of Israel, as God gave revelation to the fathers; but today there is this incredible anointing for a move of God that far exceeds the old covenant. In the past God was speaking to Israel, today he speaks to nations. The anointing has greatly increased to new levels in size, quantity, and intensity.

> *Luke 16:16 (Read also - Matthew 11:11 – 13).*
>
> *The law and the prophets were until John: since that time the kingdom of God is preached, and every man presseth into it.*

The present church age does not give a lot of credibility to Jesus the Messiah, His genuineness, authenticity and his legitimacy as to who He is, we give more credibility to Isaiah, Jeremiah, and the prophets of the Old Dispensation than to Jesus.

Several things can be derived from that:

1. The present age of Christians seems to have lost connection with the foundational principles of faith in Jesus Christ.

2. The Church has put more emphasis on what Jesus did than what he said. The central message is about his death burial resurrection and ascension. The Church's message has been to preach Christ and Him beign crucified. (Corinthians 2:2)

3. The present generation of Christians know about Jesus but don't know Jesus. It is one thing to hear of Jesus than to know Jesus, that is, to have a working, intimate relationship with Him.

Let us bring into perspective our first resource scripture, Matthew 16:13-20. *"Who do men say that I am?"* Listen to their answers; *"some say… one of the prophets."* Today it seems as if Jesus is still numbered among the prophets.

Let us call the venerable Apostle Paul to the witness stand: maybe thirty years after being saved this man of God was still praying for accurate knowledge of Christ, as seen in Philippians 3:8-10.

> *8 Yea doubtless, and I count all things but loss for the excellency of the knowledge of Christ Jesus my Lord: for whom I have suffered the loss of all things, and do count them but dung, that I may win Christ,*

> *9 And be found in him, not having mine own righteousness, which is of the law, but that which is through the faith of Christ, the righteousness which is of God by faith:*

> *10 That I may know him, and the power of his resurrection, and the fellowship of his sufferings, being made conformable unto his death;*

"EXCELLENCY OF THE KNOWLEDGE" in verse 10 with reference to today's scenario could be read like this:

> *I press, all kinds of knowledge in the education system, all kinds of interpretations in the religious organization but I press towards the mark of the high calling,*

Therefore, the credibility of the Church has been compromised by a lack of accurate knowledge of Christ; who He was and the reason that He came to the planet.

The identity of Christ is established in:

John 1:1-2

In the beginning was the Word, and the Word was with God, and the Word was God. 2The same was in the beginning with God.

Jesus is God who came to the earth as the final prophetic voice to man. He is the **last** Adam. We should pay careful attention to a very important matter that the Church has overlooked over the years, which is, the baptism of Jesus as mentioned in Matthew 3:13-17.

The Godhead assembled for the second time to execute a stupendous and awesome event - the creation of the last Adam. There was the Son in the water, the Holy Spirit coming down like a dove and the Father speaking from Heaven.

When did the first event take place? At the beginning of creation when the first man - Adam was created. The Godhead assembled and said:

> *Genesis 1:26-28. "Let us make man in our image and after our likeness;..."*

Note carefully every other creative act was by God speaking a word, but when the time came for man to come on the scene, the greatest of God's creative act, it took **US**, the coming together of the Father, Son and the Holy Spirit. **"Let us make this one" - God in an earth suit.**

Luke 16:16

16 The law and the prophets were until John: since that time the kingdom of God is preached, and every man presseth into it.

Matthew 11: 11-13.

11 Verily I say unto you, Among them that are born of women there hath not risen a greater than John the Baptist: notwithstanding he that is least in the kingdom of heaven is greater than he.

12 And from the days of John the Baptist until now the kingdom of heaven suffereth violence, and the violent take it by force.

13 For all the prophets and the law prophesied until John.

Hebrews 1:1-2

1God, who at sundry times and in divers manners spake in time past unto the fathers by the prophets, 2 <u>Hath in these last days</u> spoken unto us by his Son, whom he hath appointed heir of all things, by whom also he made the worlds;

This is Emanuel, this is the Word that is God, this the Creator, this is God speaking, not another prophet.

As mentioned earlier, these scriptures stand forever as reminders to us, that an unprecedented shift has taken place in the way God is presently dealing with people on the planet. A perfect example is the Apostle Peter's ministry, one preaching under the power of the Holy

Ghost, and 3000 souls were saved (Acts 2).

Listen carefully, God anointed Jesus and God has anointed us (2 Corinthians 1:21). Tell someone, *"you carry an anointing"*. Touch yourself and say, *"I carry an anointing. The Spirit of the Lord is upon me to bring the reality of God's world into our world to fix what is broken and disrupted by sin."*

> ***(Luke 10: 17 – 19, 21, 23)*** *[17] And the seventy returned again with joy, saying, Lord, even the devils are subject unto us through thy name. [18] And he said unto them, I beheld Satan as lightning fall from heaven. [19] Behold, I give unto you power to tread on serpents and scorpions, and over all the power of the enemy: and nothing shall by any means hurt you.*
>
> *[21] In that hour Jesus rejoiced in spirit, and said, I thank thee, O Father, Lord of heaven and earth, that thou hast hid these things from the wise and prudent, and hast revealed them unto babes: even so, Father; for so it seemed good in thy sight. [23] And he turned him unto his disciples, and said privately, Blessed are the eyes which see the things that ye see:*

We have been speaking to you about the Kingdom of God. The Kingdom of God is the theme of Jesus' teachings. All that Jesus taught and demonstrated was related to the Kingdom of God.

1. Born again - John 3: 3 - 5

2. The Church - Matthew 16:18 - 19

3. The blessings of children - Mark 10: 14 -15.

4. The casting out of demons – Matthew 12: 22 - 28

5. He said those who follow Him must preach the Kingdom of God
   - Luke 9: 60 - 62

6. He said His return is conditioned on the preaching of the gospel of the Kingdom - Matt. 24: 14

7. He used parables to teach the kingdom - Matthew 13.

8. The covenant meal, what is commonly called "the communion ". - Matthew 26:26-29.

9. When He returns, those who meet the criteria will inherit the kingdom - Matthew 25: 31-34

Is the Gospel of the kingdom any different from what you have been hearing in your church? I would answer, in some churches, yes. The message of salvation that has been preached for the past two thousand years that has at its foundation:

1. The lordship of Jesus Christ.
2. Salvation by Faith in the redemptive work of Christ on the cross.
3. The baptism in the Holy Spirit.
4. The sanctification of the believer. And whatever else that is of sound doctrine is parallel in some sense to the Kingdom of God.

The emergence of the Gospel of the Kingdom on the world stage today is to prepare the church for the return of Christ, and to give detailed information regarding the glorious Kingdom to come.

The believer must be prepared for the glorious return of Christ not to take them to heaven to live with God forever and ever as it has been taught, but through a series of divine activities set up a righteous government in the earth (Daniel 2:44).

The Gospel of the Kingdom of God will add revelation of God's plans and purpose for you and the universe. It will also help you to better understand the dimension of the supernatural with regards to all that occurs in your local church. We must shift our focus from going to heaven to live with God, to God's purpose of a glorified immortal human race. This involved living in a transformed glorious universe under the governance of God, which is the glorious future Kingdom that is our inheritance (Matthew 25:31- 34).

The Kingdom of Heaven is a vast unending glorious territory with structures of operation, various levels of authority, a place where enumerable spiritual intelligences exist in harmonious relationships in worship and obedience to the great God our savior.

It needs to be understood that the Kingdom of God, is not only governance, power, authority, it is tangible spiritual reality that carries an environment of glory. The awesome complexity of the realm of the kingdom cannot be adequately described by words. The apostle Paul in 1 Corinthians 2:9 put it this way,

> *"eyes have not seen, ears have not heard, neither has it entered*
> *into the heart of men the things God has prepared for them that*
> *love him."*

But it is just as the Scriptures say, "What God has planned for people who love him is more than eyes have seen or ears have heard. It has never even entered our minds!"   Verse 10. Says however *"but God has revealed them to us by His Spirit..".*

A kingdom perspective will make us less carnal and more spiritual. It will liberate us from cultural and earth-bound influences to a more glorious expanded understanding of God's will for the human race.

We, who are the called of God, desire to build a strong kingdom community on the revelation of the word of God, with strong prophetic insight and awareness. Prophetic insight comes from the Word of God concerning His kingdom, such as Isaiah 65 and the following scriptures:

Daniel 7:13-18,27 - I saw in the night visions, and, behold, one like the Son of man came with the clouds of heaven, and came to the Ancient of days, and they brought him near before him. **14** *And there was given him dominion, and glory, and a kingdom, that all people, nations, and languages, should serve him: his dominion is an everlasting dominion, which shall not pass away, and his kingdom that which shall not be destroyed.* **15** *I Daniel was grieved in my spirit in the midst of my body, and the visions of my head troubled me.* **16** *I came near unto one of them that stood by, and asked him the truth of all this. So he told me, and made me know the interpretation of the things.* **17** *These great beasts, which are four, are four kings, which shall arise out of the earth.* **18** *But the saints of the most High shall take the kingdom, and possess the kingdom for ever, even for ever and ever.* **27** *And the kingdom and dominion, and the greatness of the kingdom under the whole heaven, shall be given to the people of the saints of the most High, whose kingdom is an everlasting kingdom, and all dominions shall serve and obey him.*

Daniel 2:44-45 **44** *And in the days of these kings shall the God of heaven set up a kingdom, which shall never be destroyed: and the kingdom shall not be left to other people, but it shall* *break in pieces and consume all these kingdoms, and it shall stand for ever. ⁴⁵ Forasmuch as thou sawest that the stone was cut out of the mountain without hands, and that it brake in pieces the iron, the brass, the clay, the silver, and the gold; the great God hath made known to the king what shall come to pass hereafter: and the dream is certain, and the interpretation thereof sure*

Isaiah 11: 6-9 - ⁶ The wolf also shall dwell with the lamb, and the leopard shall lie down with the kid; and the calf and the young lion and the fatling together; and a little child shall lead them. ⁷ And the cow and the bear shall feed; their young ones shall lie down together: and the lion shall eat straw like the ox. ⁸ And the sucking child shall play on the hole of the asp, and the weaned child shall put his hand on the cockatrice's den. ⁹ They shall not hurt nor destroy in all my holy mountain: for the earth shall be full of the knowledge of the Lord, as the waters cover the sea.

Most denominations are founded on the understanding of some doctrine of scripture. However the Gospel of the Kingdom is distinctly different from a doctrine. Paul said the message of the Kingdom is not only in words but in power 1 Cor.4: 20. Kingdom speaks of authority, power, dominion, influence, glory, honor, splendor. It is representing God and his kingdom government in today's world. **Life on this planet is heading to one great climax. That is when all of life comes under the governance of the kingdom of God, according to Revelation 11:15.**

Revelation 11:15 - And the seventh angel sounded; and there were great voices in heaven, saying, The kingdoms of this world are become the kingdoms of our Lord, and of his Christ; and he shall reign for ever and ever.

When Jesus begun to preach the first words he uttered were "repent, for the Kingdom of Heaven is at hand". Repent means to change the way you are thinking. What you think affects how you act, and how you act determines the person that you are. Repent and change the way you are thinking. For if you change your concept your conduct will change, and your character will change. The root of a man's action lies in the way he thinks. It is his inspiration that motivates him, "for so a man thinks in his heart so is he."

Repentance does not always necessarily mean sin. It means to change your thinking. The way you think and act towards a thing or a person, etc. Before I went to bible college, I had a powerful testimony and a whole lot of zeal. This didn't go unnoticed by my pastor and others in the church I attended at that time. I was soon asked to exhort, preach, and take on other responsibilities. I was asked to preach in meetings, crusades, and other church events. I was soon known as "evangelist Rosewelt". People were coming to get saved and sanctified. When I finally went to bible college, still living in the glory of my achievements, highly respected by some of my peers, something happened after two years. I have now received new information about the ways of God: more content and detailed material from the word of God: the accomplishments of some great men of God and other substantial evidences of great spiritual significance. I began to measure what I used to preach against the knowledge I have accumulated in the past two years. I was greatly convicted of the errors and the ways I misrepresented the word of God. I wept before The Lord asking for forgiveness. It's not that I had sinned, but I was in error.

Jesus said change the way you are thinking because the Kingdom of God has just arrived on earth.

They were thinking:

> Poverty - when their focus should be Blessed (Mathew 5: 1-12; Psalm 1 & Dueteronomy 28)

> Sickness - when God had covenanted to heal them (Exodus 15:26, Psalm103, Isaiah 53:5 & Matthew 8:17. This was to fulfill what was declared by the prophet Isaiah when he said,

"It was he who took our illnesses away and removed our diseases." (ISV).

> Defeat - When they should be more than conquerors.

"...greater is He who is in you, than he that is the world" – 1 John 4:4 (KJV)

"When the enemy comes in like a flood the Spirit of the Lord lift up a standard against him" – Isaiah 59:19 (KJV)

> Weakness - when strength was ordained.

"...let the weak say I am strong" – Joel 3:10 (KJV)

Power has been sent into the earth according to Acts 1:8, that you can access.

> Going to heaven- what work in Heaven has just come to earth.

"Thy kingdom come thy will be done on earth as in heaven" – Matthew 6:10 (KJV)

DEFINITIONS OF THE KINGDOM:

While the Kingdom of God has to do with governance, with laws and decrees, ordinance, and various systems of operation, it also comes with an environment of glory and power.

1. The Kingdom of God is where the unseen spiritual world ruled by God breaks in, or invades the visible physical world bringing salvation, deliverance for the people of God, it also brings order to a disordered life.

2. The Kingdom of God is that invisible spiritual realty that has tremendous capabilities to impact and influence the visible physical realm.

3. The Kingdom of Heaven is that spiritual realm existing in the heavenly realms where the sovereign rule of God is carried out.

4. It is the realm where God dominates - His system of governance.

5. The Kingdom is the operation of the the power, influence, and dominance of God.

6. The Kingdom of God is the operation of God's power within His domain. "Thy Kingdom come thy will be done on Earth as in Heaven" Heaven is the sphere/realm of the operation of the Kingdom. For God's will to be done in the Heavens the exertion of His kingdom's influence and power must go into operation. For God's will to be done on earth His kingdom influence and power must be exerted on Earth.

7. The Government of God: The Kingship of God: The rule

of God: The Divine order of God.

8. The Kingdom of God is the restoration of God's order on the earth.

9. Jesus came to restore a lost order. He came to seek and to save that which was lost.

The operation of God's power is seen:

1. In Him creating a people by the new birth (2 Corinthians 5:17).

2. By bringing them into a realm in which His power is experienced (the new birth brings you into the Kingdom of God) John 3:3-5 & Colossians 1:13

3. People of the Kingdom are those who submit to the rule of God in their lives.

4. One of the questions we wish to answer is where is the Kingdom? Jesus said "the kingdom is at hand". He meant it has arrived, you can access it, interact with it, you can experience its power and influence. You can receive from its power. Where is the Kingdom? It's right here - a spiritual dimension from you.

5. Jesus said "If I cast out devils by the Spirit of God then the Kingdom has come upon you". St. Matthew 12:28

6. John the apostle said in the book of Revelation 1: 9 - He is in the Kingdom.

The Kingdom is viewed from three aspects:

Actual	It is present, right here! Matt. 12: 28

Ideal	It is to come in its political operations on the planet
Moral	It is the rule of God in the heart. Morality is interpreted as the power to do what is right. This means you have the power of God in you to do what is right. Luke 17: 20 - 21 Psalm 119:11 "thy word have I hidden in my heart that I might not sin against you." Ps. 23: "...you lead me in the paths of righteousness for thy name sake". Jesus has never taught that you should get holy, neither did he commend the very holy and said they will find a place in the kingdom. He said," Seek he first the Kingdom of God and his righteousness, and all other things will be added unto you." Righteousness is not something you do. Righteousness is what you are. God is righteous. The righteousness which is of God. "Holiness unto the Lord is a watch word and song" Holiness is not a watch word and song, it is a life to be lived. Holiness is not the attribute of God it is the nature of God. Therefore, since God said, "Be Holy for I am Holy," you are to be. Holiness is being. When you are born again God's nature was given to you. Jesus was never amazed if one looks holy, if you have the nature of the holy one you are holy. Jesus would be very astonished if you are not. How do you follow holiness? By expressing

the divine nature! The nature will produce what the scripture calls the fruit of the Spirit. When we were born again, regenerated, a new principle of life was introduced into our dead bankrupt human spirit that produces a whole new pattern of behavior. This is not about physical changes

"for the Kingdom of God is not meat or drink it is righteousness peace and joy in the Holy Spirit." Romans 14:17

"Christ in you the hope of Glory" (Colossians 1:27) what is in us is changing from glory to glory

"we have a treasure in earthen vessel" - 2 Cor. 3: 17

7. KINGDOM REPLACEMENT

The present world system will be replaced by God's Kingdom government as a divine interposition arresting the process of the present world syste, reversing all the evil therein"

This Dispensation. (A specific system by which something is dispensed or authorized)

> ***Matthew 19:28 (KJV)*** *And Jesus said unto them, Verily I say unto you, That ye which have followed me, in the regeneration when the Son of man shall sit in the throne of his glory, ye also shall sit upon twelve thrones, judging the twelve tribes of Israel.*

> ***Ephesians 1:10*** *That in the dispensation of the fulness of times he might gather together in one all things in Christ, both which are in heaven, and which are on earth; even in him: (KJV)*

Other scriptures include:

- Mark 10:30;
- Luke 18:30.
- Ephesians 1:21.
- Hebrews 6:4-5.
- Luke 16: 16
- Matthew 11:11-13

The number one problem in today's church is identity crisis. The church doesn't know who she is. The people in the church believe the church is a bride, or sheep, that is as a result of what is preached with great exuberance from the pulpit, analogy, typology & metaphors. The church has become weak, timid, defenseless, but the message of the Kingdom says, "the kingdom suffers violence but the violent take it by force".

This misunderstanding of what the church is, its mission and God given assignment has given rise to a backward knowledge of Christ.

Identity Crisis is defined as: *A psychosocial state of disorientation and role confusion occurring especially in adolescents as a result of conflicting internal and external experiences, pressures, and expectations which often produce acute anxiety.* (Wikipedia).

Some people believe that you are not who you say you are if you do not wear a hat, if you don't attend church on a specific, then there is the dress in white, and countless other details. Anxious to leave the world and go to Heaven and rest; the church has allowed the world to define them, as a result the world has expectations of the church that God knows nothing about.

❖ The church is not a religious organization as defined by the governments of the world and some religious organizations.

❖ The church is the executive arm of the kingdom of Heaven. So, the church is not the kingdom. The church was created by the kingdom government of God.

❖ The church has the keys of the kingdom. Keys are symbolic to authority.

Note carefully that the church was never intended to be a religious organization. The church is a governmental agency that is given authority over the earth. The church is given the "Keys" of the kingdom. Given the authority of the government of God.

> *Mat 16:18 And I say also unto thee, That thou art Peter, and upon this rock I will build my church; and the gates of hell shall not prevail against it.*
>
> *Mat 16:19 And I will give unto thee the keys of the kingdom of heaven: and whatsoever thou shalt bind on earth shall be bound in heaven: and whatsoever thou shalt loose on earth shall be loosed in heaven.*

One profound truth revealed in this statement is life on earth is governed from the heavens.

REDEFINE THE CHURCH

Church is not a religious word. The word *ecclesia* originated with the Greeks and was used by the Romans. Church (*ecclesia*) is a called-out people given authority by the government in the different Roman provinces, implementing the collective policies of the government of Rome. The church Jesus Christ created is the executive arm of the government of God on the earth. That's why Jesus had to give the church the keys (authority) of the kingdom of heaven. What is the assignment of the church? The assignment of the church is incredible and of great importance.

Apart from binding and loosing, allow and disallow the church exercise dominion and influence in the earth, the church also wrestled against principalities and power, rulers of darkness and spiritual wickedness in high places. Ephesians 6: 12 -18. The church in its present organized state does not wrestle against flesh and blood.   The church is the agency used by God to instruct the cosmic intelligences of the manifold wisdom of God (Ephesians 3:10). The range of dominion and influence of the church is on earth. Man has no influence in Heaven. God is already the absolute king of heaven. If man is going to be kings and lords it could not be in heaven. Two kings cannot reign in the same territory. The most awesome being ever created by God is man: from the time he created Adam and gave Adam His nature all other created beings were looking at God in an earth suit. If you don't understand, then a study or examination of the life of Jesus Christ should bring illumination.

How you disciple/train the reconciled, believers? In other words, how do you bring the community of the saved to their true identity, to progress to a higher degree in Christ? The present expression is making the church irrelevant to the age, people outside of the church can predict the behavior of people inside the church. Anybody can play church. For example, on the Internet there are videos of homosexual churches. They have everything you have in your church – pastor, pulpit, chairs, bible, musical instruments, praise and worship, people getting in the spirit, the taking of communion, etc. The unenlightened are in confusion, because they see the same thing in other places of worship.

Most churches have one commonality, whether, it's the homosexual church, wrap-head, Saturday, or Sunday they have one common goal, they are all going off to heaven to live with God. That's the goal, the objective, the mind set.

Goals provide the energy source that powers our lives. Its our motivation, it drives us. Unless the church refocuses its energy from going to heaven to sing and shout and dance about, to the kingdom government of God that is to be established in the universe, we will be expending energy on multitude of activities that not only are redundant, but make us irrelevant as a church in the earth.

It's not that we are not teaching, preaching, counseling, evangelizing, having crusades, conferences, etc., but all these "activities" are not bearing any visible fruit for the Kingdom. For example, according to the Guiness Book of World Records™, Jamaica has the most churches per square mile. Yet, we still have 86% of children born outside of wedlock, there is an escalation of violence, we are on the verge of legalizing the abomination of homosexuality. We are an undeveloped country due to a brain drain going off to "heaven" in North America. It is an indictment against the church that this is so because we are misaligned with the principles that govern the Kingdom of God.

The teaching that "its all about going to heaven as the ultimate goal" has caused multitudes going to church to miss 'opportunities and neglect responsibilities, promote poverty, and live in ignorance of the plans and purposes of God for the human race and by extension the universe. If we think we have the antivirus and it's not working, we can conclude that we are using the wrong antivirus. The teaching of going to heaven to live with God as the ultmate goal of the church is not supportable by scripture.

Have you ever considered why one man's disobedience has caused calamitous destructive consequences to the human race? What Adam did, affected everything on the planet. The truth is Adam didn't just sin. His action was an act of rebellion against a Government - God's kingdom government. He was incited by Satan to carry out an act of treason against the government of God to which he was aligned.

Adam's relationship to the king and His kingdom was above and beyond that of the angels. Adam was the offspring of the King of heaven. He would carry the very nature of God. He was the King's son. (Luke 3:38) He was given a domain, a territory over which he would have rulership, dominion. Consider this carefully, if Adam did not declare independence from God and His kingdom, he would be filled with all the attributes of God. These attributes are love,

If the God you serve is one that is trying to help you escape earth to live in heaven with him forever and ever, then you have missed the God of the Kingdom of God.

wisdom, holiness, righteousness, goodness, power, might, glory, honor: Ephesians 3:18-20. (Rev. 5:12.). We would not be preaching holiness since all would be holy.

However, in the process of his development to be filled with all the fullness of God, he fell. He declared independence from God and his kingdom. Paul the ambassador of the kingdom described the fall as, "all have sinned and come short of the glory (which is the fullness) of God". Romans 3:24.

> *"Therefore, as by one man sin entered the world and death by sin so death has passed upon all men for all have sinned. Roman 5:12.*

How do you disciple the reconciled? How do you bring about a paradigm shift in people's thinking and behavior? The church must have a shift in goals and objectives and get back to the original blueprint, which is the word of God.

Now hold on to your stones, I am about to ask a question. When was it that God said he created man to come and live with him in heaven? Where in the original foundation did the Lord Jesus say, "repent for I have come to take you to heaven?"

Our Lord did not say that to His disciples, He could not have said it to the generation to which He came, because God promised to the Jewish nation a glorious kingdom right here on earth. Search the prophets, especially in Daniel 2: 44-45. 7:24-27. The Bible says, "the saint shall possess the kingdom"

Israel as a nation today is not impressed by Christianity neither can today's church effectively witness to Israel, because the church's Messiah is not Israel's Messiah. Israel expects a Messiah who is going to set up a kingdom on earth, not one to take them to live in heaven forever and ever.

There are foundational scriptures that support this:

- Daniel 2:37-49; 7:14, 22
- Matt. 4:17-23; 5:3,10,19,20; 6:10,33; 8:11,12; 9:35
- Matt. 10:7
- Matthew 11:11-12
- Matthew 13

What you choose to focus your mind on is critical because you will become what you think about most of the time. We as the church must refocus our minds from going to heaven and rest, to focus on the next dispensation that God is about to bring about in the earth with a mighty display of power and glory. (Theologians refer to that as the second coming of Christ).

a. *Dispensation: The divine ordering of worldly affairs.*
A supernatural system of events, structures of governance, various affairs such as politics economy and other matters related to earth and its inhabitants considered to have been divinely revealed or appointed.

Reference to that Dispensation can be found in:

- Matthew 19:28,
- Ephesians 1:10;

- Mark 10:30;
- Luke 18:30.
- Ephesians 1:21
- Hebrews 2:v5; 6:v5

"God spoke in time past by the prophets" – Hebrew 1:1 God speaks and carries out his purpose in various dispensations.

There was the dispensation of the first kingdom under Adam and Eve, there was the dispensation of law, we are now in the dispensation of Grace/Holy Spirit, the next dispensation is that of the Kingdom of God as a glorious organized system of governance in the universe, of which Jesus will be King of kings and Lord of lords.

It will be the ultimate state of glory and happiness. The manifest powers of that age will be evident by the immortality, incorruption, and the glory of the human body, the spirits of righteous people made perfect (Hebrews 12:23). The entire freedom from all evils of every kind, no more temptation, trial, test, sorrow, we will have full unbroken communion with Father, Son, and Spirit, and a complete enjoyment of all happiness forever; when God brings all things together under Christ.

God has created worlds, structures and systems of operations, there are principalities, thrones, dominions, powers. He has also created visible things and invisible things: things seen and unseen. These include solar systems and galaxies, stars and moons and time n space. God has created enumerable spiritual intelligences that worship and obey him.

If the God you serve is one that is trying to help you escape earth to live in heaven with him forever and ever, then you have missed the God of the Kingdom of God.

8. PRAYER POINTS FOR KINGDOM ACTIVATION

There is a world that is well structured, highly organized, filled with enumerable spiritual intelligences, supernatural in its operations, an unseen spiritual reality that is keenly interested in the people living on this planet called Earth.

> *Psalm 145:11-13.* - *11 They shall speak of the glory of thy kingdom, and talk of thy power; 12 To make known to the sons of men his mighty acts, and the glorious majesty of his kingdom. 13 Thy kingdom is an everlasting kingdom, and thy dominion endureth throughout all generations.*

So great is the interest and deep the concerns that someone from that world was sent to our world with the greatest message of hope to Earth dwellers. This was a message of redemption and salvation for the restoring of relationship to a Heavenly Father, and the reconnection to a kingdom that mankind has lost, the Kingdom of God.

It is the invasion of God's world to fix what is broken and dysfunctional in our world.

By definition the Kingdom of God is an invisible spiritual reality that has incredible power and great influence, to invade and impact the visible material world to bring about incredible changes in conformity to the will of God on behalf of the believers.

It is also vast, of a degree above measures, realm, area, sphere of influence and power where there is no death, darkness, disaster, sin, sickness, or weakness. Divine restoration and instant replenishment are laws that operate in The Kingdom of God. Life cannot be suspended in God's kingdom, that is why only in this Kingdom you can and will ever have eternal life.

For example, when we pray for any matter whether it is for the sick, circumstances to change, or for salvation/deliverance it is the releasing of the Kingdom power and influence of God into that given situation. It is the invasion of God's world to fix what is broken and dysfunctional in our world.

From the very beginning of his ministry until the day of his ascension our Lord Jesus had one message, the Kingdom of God or the kingdom from heaven. It's unfortunate that the present-day church has no idea about the kingdom of heaven, the very message they were told to preach.

The inheritance of the human race is the Kingdom of God – (Matthew 25: 31-34). Jesus said to His disciples:

- it is the Father's good pleasure to give you the kingdom (Luke 12:32)

- When the Son of man shall come in his glory, and all the holy angels with him, then shall he sit upon the throne of his glory (Matthew 25:31)

- Then shall the King say unto them on his right hand, Come, ye blessed of my Father, inherit the kingdom prepared for you from the foundation of the world (Matthew 25:34)

Just as Satan's kingdom is infested and operate through demonic activities, the operations of the Kingdom God is through angels sent on assignment by God.

PRAYERS FOR KINGDOM ACTIVATION

Because I am born of God and have entered His Kingdom, I am seated above principalities and power. I possess the keys of the kingdom to bind and to loose in the name of the Lord Jesus (Ephesians 2: 5-6). Kingdom authority has been given to me and great privileges because of my union with Christ Jesus my Lord.

1. I pursue, I overtake, and I recover all that the enemy has robbed by deception from my life, and ministry in the name of the Lord Jesus Christ and by the power of God.

2. Because I seek first the Kingdom of God and His righteousness all other things are added unto me.

3. Thank You Father that You have translated me into the kingdom of Your beloved Son with all rights and privileges for great success (Colossians 1:13)

4. I decree and declare that I am blessed and highly favored by God.

5. Because I am divinely positioned in God's kingdom all curses against me are cancelled and I receive a hundredfold blessing of all I undertake to do, in the name of Jesus.

6. As a citizen of the Kingdom of God, and a believer of God's word, nothing shall be impossible for me. For all things are possible for them that believe (Mark 9:23).

7. I declare as a joint heir with the Messiah Jesus that I am for signs and for wonders in the earth, to the glory of my God, in Jesus' name.

8. Lord let the supernatural and miraculous operations of Your kingdom manifest in my life and ministry to astonish my enemies.

9. In the name of the Lord Jesus, and as joint heir with Christ I decree that every valley shall rise up and every crooked path be made straight before me as I advance in God's kingdom government

10. Because I am born again and carry God's DNA, angels are on assignment to my life and ministry for protection, provision and for making special arrangements for my success.

11. Sovereign Lord let me walk constantly in the glory of Thy kingdom.

12. Sovereign Lord let Your Kingdom wreak havoc upon them that set themselves against me.

13. On the authority of Your word I declare Thine is the kingdom the power and the glory, in Jesus' name.

14. Sovereign Lord deliver me from every evil work and convey me into your heavenly kingdom, in Jesus' name (2 Timothy 4:18)

15. Great God my savior manifest Your kingdom power on my behalf destroying all evil oppositions to my life, my ministry and my family, in the name of the Lord Jesus Christ

16. Sovereign Lord let your kingdom power invade the dominion of darkness and make room for me to prosper.

17. Lord let divine invasion of your kingdom create turbulence in the dominion of darkness and give me a clear path to my purpose and destiny, in Jesus' name

18. Sovereign Lord as I praise you let the glory of Your kingdom appear to set ambush against my enemies to fight among themselves, in Jesus' name (2 Chronicles 20:22)

19. Holy Father Lord let Your Kingdom come so that Your will be done in the earth as it is done in heaven, in Jesus' name.

20. Holy Father revisit the foundation of my life to re-arrange and repair any weaknesses, cracks or faults, that give any place to the devil, in Jesus' name.

21. Sovereign Lord let Your glorious Kingdom rule on my behalf to fulfill my assignment successfully in the earth, in Jesus' name.

22. Sovereign Lord let your glorious Kingdom rule on my behalf to carry out my assignment in the earth in excellence

23. Jehovah El Shaddai, the covenant keeping God let the blessing of Abraham come upon me that I may inherit your heavenly kingdom, in Jesus' name (Galatians 3:14)

24. Father God let your Holy Spirit begin to minister to me now manifesting my kingdom authority (Matthew 16:19).

25. Holy Spirit minister to my spirit, minister to my mind, minister to my body, in Jesus' name (John 14:17)

26. Holy Spirit greater one who lives in me manifest your kingdom power and glory on my behalf (1 Corinthians 4:20)

27. Sovereign Lord as I seek first Your Kingdom let everything necessary to fulfill my assignment be supernaturally added unto me, in Jesus' name.

28. Let Your kingdom within me rise up to deny and restrict any satanic access to my life (Luke 17:21).

29. In the name of the Lord Jesus I receive divine thoughts, revelations, visions, insights, wisdom and understanding from the kingdom within me (Luke 17:21)

30. In the name of the Lord Jesus, I bind and prohibit the devil from stealing the word of the Kingdom from my heart I am destined to bring forth fruits a hundredfold (Matthew 13:19)

31. Heavenly Father according to the riches of Your glory grant a strengthening of those things that reinforce my kingdom authority and establish me in heavenly places.

32. Holy Spirit great God my helper, perform on my behalf bringing to fulfillment every prophetic word over my life and Ministry.

33. In the name of the Lord Jesus let my body come in divine alignment to the word of God and function according to divine protocol, "As it is written, he took my sicknesses and carried my diseases with his wounds I am healed".

34. Great God my Savior let Your Kingdom begin to operate mightily on my behalf to contain the dominion of darkness and confine them to useless, ineffective and futile activities over my ministry, my life, my family and my finances.

35. Holy Spirit Reveal to me the mysteries of the kingdom of Heaven (Matthew 13:11).

36. Lord of Host create turbulence, make re-arrangement, revision, reorganization and re-routing of situations and circumstances to give a clear path to my desired miracles.

37. Because I am a citizen of the Kingdom of God I am empowered to bind, to loose, to decree a thing and it is established. I am fully authorized because I am under the authority of the king.

38. Thank you Lord for Your Kingdom that is within me, let your kingdom within me prohibit all limitations to my success and accomplishments.

39. Great God establish the boundaries, parameters and borders of Your Kingdom around me and govern all activities within to be in conformity to Your divine will.

40. Holy Spirit as I worship create the environment of Your Kingdom around me with every divine element and influence, power and glory.

41. Sovereign Lord help me make known to the nations Your mighty works and the glorious majesty and splendor of Your Kingdom (Psalm 145:12)

42. Your Kingdom is from everlasting and Your dominion from one generation to another (Psalm 145:13)

43. Let me be a nation changer through the revelation of Your Kingdom and a manifestation of Your power and Your glory, in Jesus' name.

44. I receive Your Kingdom for it is Your good pleasure to give it to me, therefore I declare thine is the kingdom, mine is the kingdom (Luke 12:32)

45. In the name of Jesus Christ let kingdom power be released on my behalf to regulate satanic and demonic activities to uselessness.

46. Father God let the righteousness of Your Kingdom its peace and joy in the Holy Ghost be established in my life (Romans 14:17)

47. In the name of The Lord Jesus I relentlessly pursue the Kingdom and forcefully press into it (Luke 16:16)

48. Father God give me understanding to possess the Kingdom as Your word says the Saints shall posses the Kingdom (Daniel 7:18-27).

49. As a citizen of the Kingdom of God I declare to principalities and power that no weapon formed against me shall prosper and every tongue rise against me in judgement is condemned this is my heritage.

50. Holy Spirit as we worship manifest the environment of the kingdom around us with its divine influence, power and glory.

51. Holy Father according to the riches of Your glory strengthen me with might by Your Spirit in my inner man, let there be

no lack of the divine deposits You ordained for me in Christ Jesus (Ephesians 3:16).

NOTE

> ***Proverbs 11:11*** *- By the blessing of the upright the city is exalted: but it is overthrown by the mouth of the wicked.*

Let us therefore speak blessings over our city.

KINGDOM POWER.

John 3:3-10.

The great Creator, the one through whom all things exist, appeared on the planet over 2000 years ago with a message to earth dwellers. A message of hope, a comprehensive revelation of who we are; the greatest and most incredible message about a father who loved us and a kingdom for us to connect to (John 3:16). But men chose their religion to make them comfortable rather than try to understand the incredible and awesome revelation of the message of the Kingdom of Heaven.

The bible teaches that the Kingdom of God is God's power in operation. The apostle Paul wrote in 1 Corinthians 4:*20 "for the Kingdom of God is not in word, but in power"*. Jesus taught his disciples to pray and to request of the Father that *"the Kingdom of God will come to earth, that his will be done in the earth as it is done in the heaven"*. The prayer ends with the declaration, *"Thine is the Kingdom, the Power and the Glory"*.

God's power is considered supernatural, that is, operating outside the scope of the natural world. For example, death is the natural outcome to human life over a process of time it would take a supernatural power to reverse death. Kingdom power is supernatural. It is the manifestation of a process of operation beyond human ability.

Often in services where the presence and power of God is overwhelmingly evident, people would say that the power of God moved in the service. We now know that it is Kingdom power or the Kingdom of God that is in operation. This power invades the dominion of darkness and deliver sinners from satanic and demonic control. This power heals the sick, ushers believers to new levels of joy, peace, and from oppressive and stressful circumstances, and situations, evidenced by the supernatural and the miraculous. Jesus said it this way, *if I by the Spirit of God I cast out devils then the Kingdom of God has come upon you.*

When people are set free from demonic control it is the result of Kingdom power manifesting through the Holy Spirit. The Holy Spirit contains all the operations of the Kingdom of God. For example when we pray for any matter whether it is for the sick, circumstances to become more favorable or for salvation/deliverance, it is the releasing of the kingdom power and influence of God in that given situation, it is the invasion of God's world into our world to fix what's broken and dysfunctional in our world. Say these prayer points audibly, with deliberation and intensity and the God of the Kingdom of Heaven will invade your world to fix what's broken or dysfunctional.

1. Sovereign Lord my God let the power of Thy Kingdom manifest on my behalf to destroy the works of darkness from affecting my life.

2. "You are my King, O God: command deliverances for Me and my household (Psalm 44:4)

3. By the power of the blood of the great God my Savior I release myself from all generational curses and iniquities as a result of the sins of my parents.

4. That You would bless me indeed, and that You would enlarge my borders, and increase the range of Your influences through me. In Jesus's name.

5. Let Your Kingdom manifest with great power as we bear witness to The Lord Jesus and declare Your salvation to nations.

6. Create the environment of Your kingdom in this place and let there be visibly manifestation of Your power and Your glory (Isaiah 60.1).

7. Let Your kingdom influence, Your power and Your glory increase in my life and over my household.

8. Let Your kingdom breakdown all barriers remove all obstacles set up by the enemy around my life and my ministry.

9. For the kingdom is the LORD'S: and he is the governor over all the nations (Psalm 22:28)

10. Sovereign Lord by the power of Your Kingdom overrule all undermining activities by the dominion of darkness that is set against me, my ministry and my household.

11. Great God my King, assign mighty angels from Your angelic host to shut down all satanic oppositions, resistance to my life, my ministry and my family.

12. How great is Your Kingdom O God, let the majestic glory fill my life, my place of worship and my dwelling.

13. In the name of the great God my Savior and by the power of His Kingdom I destabilize and render powerless all territorial spirits opposing my assignment in the earth.

14. In the name of the Lord Jesus and by the power of His Kingdom government let all enemy reinforcements against me be completely disbanded and scattered.

15. As God's authority on this earth I authorized the Kingdom of God to plunder and dismantle satanic strongholds over my life , my family, my ministry, my money.

16. Holy Spirit great God my helper, take from the reservoir of divine deposit in me to make unmistakably clear Your glory and Your power.

17. Let all satanic contentions, provocations and intentions concerning my life, my health, my money or any family members be incarcerated restricted by angels sent from the Kingdom of God.

18. As ambassador of the Kingdom of God let all the divine resources for my office begin to manifest.

19. Holy Spirit great God my helper cause me to operate at a higher level in revelations of the mysteries of the Kingdom of God (Matthew 13:11).

20. Holy Father let Your Kingdom rise up in me to eliminate ungodly worry, completely remove fear and false burdens from my life (Matthew 13:11)

21. The Lord will crush my enemies before me and strike all those who hate me (Psalm 89:23).

22. As a citizen of God's Kingdom, I am divinely protected and provided for as it is written, *if I seek first the Kingdom of God and His righteousness all other things will be added unto me* (Matthew 6:33).

23. Father God as it is written, *You have made us kings and priests and we shall reign on the earth* (Revelation 5:10).

24. By the power of God's anointing on my life I terminate and abort all demonic activities against my prayer life, in the name of the lord Jesus.

25. Holy Spirit invest holy fire in my prayers to destroy demons out of my environment.

26. As God's ambassador in this region I make request that my government will assign angels to incarcerate and terminate the activities of the ruler of darkness over my city and my community. (Call the name of city/community), in the name of the Lord Jesus

27. As joint heir with Christ I request of my Father to assign legions of angels to increase their operations on my behalf against the kingdom of Satan.

28. Sovereign Lord Jesus, increase upon me the power of the Holy Spirit that mighty works will manifest in my ministry.

29. By the power of the cross of Christ I crucify my flesh from lust and evil desires, as it is written, *I am crucified with Christ nevertheless I live, yet not I but Christ that lives in me..* (Galatians 2:20).

30. In the name of the Lord Jesus Christ I request of my Father to command angels from the Kingdom of Heaven to execute judgment on the dominion of darkness that is against my life, my family and my ministry.

31. I request power of a fresh anointing to operate at a higher level in the Kingdom of God for great accomplishments and high achievements.

32. As Your Kingdom government increases in the earth let there be visible manifestations of Your power and Your glory.

33. Sovereign Lord sprinkle the blood of Christ upon my marriage that it be cleansed from any demonic or satanic agents, elements or influence.

34. Let the prophetic word of divine unity be established in my marriage for the release of dominion power, in the name of the Lord Jesus (Matthew 18:20)

35. Great God my helper imbue me with divine wisdom and make me of a good understanding in all Your ways.

36. Thy saint shall speak of the glory of Thy Kingdom and shall declare thy power to nations, let this prophetic word be activated in my life and ministry (Ps. 145:11)

37. As a legal representative of the Kingdom government of God I declare and make known to nations Your mighty acts, and the glorious majesty of Your Kingdom (Psalm 145:12)

38. Thank You Holy Father for the greater one who lives in me. For when the enemy comes in like a flood the Holy Spirit in whom are realms of the kingdom shall lift up a standard against him.

39. As a portal and door of access to God's kingdom government I bring divine resources of deliverance to nations.

40. Sovereign Lord let Your Kingdom within me manifest to Your praise and glory in the earth.

About the Author

 Bishop Dr. Frank Rosewelt is the Founder, President, Visionary and Senior Pastor of International Worship Center & Faith Ministries, along with his darling wife Hope, who is the Associate Pastor. Dr. Rosewelt has ministered both as a Pastor and Evangelist for over 17 years, carrying out pastoral duties for over 10 years in 2 mainline denominations. He has also ministered extensively in revival services both in and out of Jamaica. The gifts of Healing and the working of Miracles have become very prominent in his ministry.

Dr. Rosewelt studied at the Caribbean Wesleyan Bible College where he obtained a Diploma in Theology. In 2005 he was honored with a Doctor of Divinity Degree from the Emmanuel University in Raleigh, North Carolina, USA. His passion is teaching and preaching the Gospel of the Kingdom of God becoming a living reality in the lives of individuals and as a glorious reality to be set up in the universe.

Pastors Frank & Hope minister to a congregation of over 450 residents of Montego Bay and its environs: The Healing and Deliverance ministry held Tuesdays at 6.00 p.m., see people who are oppressed, depressed, abused, broken-hearted, broke, busted and frustrated, come to experience the life changing power of God. Many are the testimonies of healing and deliverance from various sicknesses, diseases and demonic oppression, as the mighty and powerful works of God truly authenticate the ministers and ministry.

The ministry is located in Montego Bay, Jamaica. Their television program "a Taste of The Kingdom" is broadcast on TVJ every Saturday morning at 7:00 a.m. Their services are also broadcast on the Spy Cable Network three times per week and MTM Television.

Dr. and Mrs. Rosewelt reside in Montego Bay and have been married for the past 28 years. Their union has produced 2 daughters, Joanna and Debrah-Ann.

Contact information:
Email: raisingthebarofmusic@gmail.com
Telephone: (876) 919-5268